Eat the Watermelon . . . Spit out the Seeds!

A Biography of Pastor Charles J. Petit

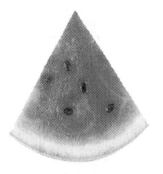

THERESA GRAY-PETIT

WESTBOW
PRESS
A DIVISION OF THOMAS NELSON

WestBow Press books may be ordered through booksellers or by contacting:

WestBow Press
A Division of Thomas Nelson
1663 Liberty Drive
Bloomington, IN 47403
www.westbowpress.com
1-(866) 928-1240

ISBN: 978-1-4497-9113-1 (sc)
ISBN: 978-1-4497-9115-5 (hc)
ISBN: 978-1-4497-9114-8 (e)

Library of Congress Control Number: 2013906384

Printed in the United States of America.

WestBow Press rev. date: 4/26/2013

Scripture taken from the King James Version of the Bible.

This Book is Dedicated To:

My son Del Anthony Gray
Del's wife Tina, and
My remarkable granddaughter, Rayne

My Stepchildren:
Cinda
Ginger
Carrie Jane
Shelly
Tessi
Sam
Crystal
Dustin
In Loving Memory of John (1966-1995)

We thank God for our children, grandchildren
(especially Trevin Paul) and great-grandchildren.

Table of Contents

Introduction

This book is a biography of my husband, Charles J. Petit. The information was obtained from his family and friends. The book also contains my personal observations and knowledge of his life.

I encourage you to read this biography of Pastor Charles J. Petit with a loving spirit, an understanding mind and a forgiving heart. Some of the information may be faded due to the passage of time, but we hope that you are encouraged and uplifted as you read this account of his life.

I want to thank Pastor Earl Mills for planting the idea for the title in my mind. One day I was discussing the positive and negative aspects of a church service with Pastor Mills. He smiled pleasantly, and with his soft gentle voice he said, "Eat the watermelon . . . spit out the seeds." Pastor Earl and Mert Mills are retired from pastoring in Pikeville, Kentucky. They are true and dear friends of ours.

A true friend knows all about you and still loves you in spite of your mistakes and failures.

"A friend loveth at all times . . ."
Proverbs 17:17 KJV

Chapter 1

Where It All Began – Hootie Preaches to Chickens

(14) But Jesus said, Suffer little children, and forbid them not, to come unto me: for of such is the Kingdom of Heaven.

Matthew 19:14 KJV

In Columbus, Ohio, a few years after the depression of 1929, a son was born into the Petit family. His father, Charles Petit, Sr., was nearly fifty (50) years old. He was so excited and extremely happy to have a son after all those years. He walked down Woodrow Avenue handing out cigars, proudly announcing the birth of his new baby boy. His chest was sticking out so far the buttons nearly burst off his shirt. He named his baby boy Charles Jr.

Junior's father was a skilled glass blower, and his mother was a homemaker who had been left a widow with eight children before she married Charles Sr.

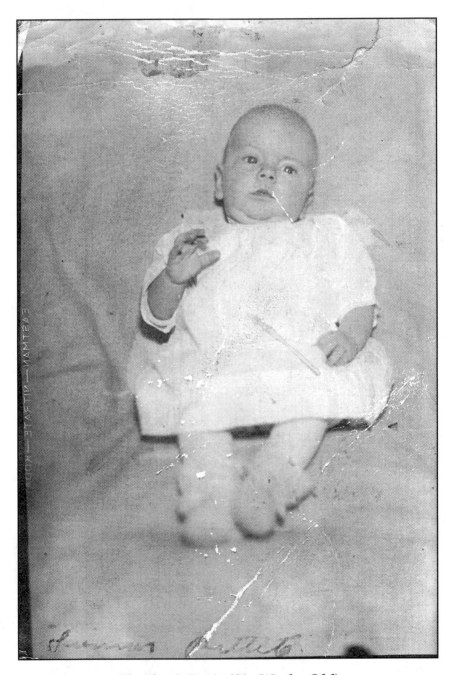

Charles J. Petit (Six Weeks Old)

Charles J. Petit, Sr. (Dad) and Georgia Petit (Mom)

A few years after Junior was born, another son came into the Petit family. There were now ten (10) children – seven boys and three girls.

Weston, West Virginia, became the next home for the Petit family, as they moved there when Junior was less than a month old. His father moved the family there in pursuit of the glass trade.

Charles Jr. (Age 2)
Weston, West Virginia

In 1939, the Petit family moved to Chillicothe, Ohio, where Charles's father became a poultry farmer. As a small child, the family attached a nickname onto Charles Jr., calling him "Hootie."

As small children, the Petit boys were raised in the Catholic church. Their father was Catholic, and their mother was Southern Baptist.

During the Chillicothe years, a neighbor, Mrs. Grace Irvin, introduced the boys to the Pilgrim Holiness Church. Grace recently passed away at age 101.

Hootie took such an interest in the "new, exciting church," that when he and his niece, Betty, were in the yard playing, they would play church, and Hootie would stand on an old orange crate and preach, pretending that he was Reverend Pugh, the pastor of the Pilgrim Holiness Church.

According to Hazel, Hootie's sister and the mother of his niece Betty, the two children would conduct church services right there in the yard among the chickens. Hootie would preach "hell, fire and brimstone," and Betty would tend the flock, trying to persuade them to listen to Pastor Hootie. Betty was about five years old, and Pastor Hootie was about six or seven years old. They would raise their hands and praise the Lord, and the chickens would cackle, "I'll Fly Away."

Left to right: Larry (Age 3), Charles Jr. (Age 5)
Chillicothe, Ohio

Pastor Pugh (background) and the
Chillicothe Sunday School Class
Charles "Pastor Hootie" (front and center with suit on)
He always liked to be front and center back then.

That may sound humorous, but that was actually the first time in Charles's life when he felt the "calling" of God to preach the Gospel.

I believe that when God places a calling upon one's life to preach the Gospel, that calling often becomes apparent very early in life. There is a young pastor in Hamilton, Ohio, named Paul Albert Hensley. He told me about a time when he was a young boy cutting grass in his backyard. As he was pushing the lawn mower along, he just began preaching.

The neighbor yelled across the fence, "What's going on, Paul Albert?"

Paul simply said, "Oh, I'm just preaching."

I believe that was a supernatural encounter with the Spirit of the Lord preparing him for the future. He has a powerful anointing of God in his life, and I believe he loves the Lord with all of his heart.

The genuine calling to preach the Gospel manifests itself as a strong desire that burns within one's soul to please God by leading the lost to Christ and keeping souls out of the flames of hell. This calling is not to be taken lightly. It must be cherished, honored, cultivated, protected and pursued with one's entire being in order to become successful and pleasing to God.

When Charles was twelve years old, the family was relocated to Washington, Pennsylvania. He and his younger brother, Larry, attended the Lutheran Church at the request of their father. They were confirmed Lutheran at fourteen and twelve years old, respectively. It was in the Lutheran Church that Charles was taught the importance of studying the Word of God. The Word became very real to him and valuable to his "calling" in life.

The Petit work ethic kicked in for Charles while they lived in Washington, Pennsylvania. Charles started selling newspapers. He stood on the street corner in town and yelled, "Pittsburgh Press, Sun Telly Papers!" He loved being the center of attention and meeting new people.

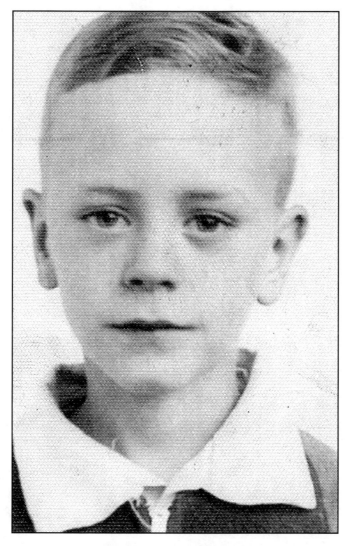

Charles J. Petit (Age 9)

Left to right: Charles Jr., Charles Sr.,
Georgia (Mom), Larry (Brother)
Washington, Pennsylvania, Easter Sunday in the late 40's
Charles and his brother Larry were confirmed Lutheran.

Even as a child, Charles could make conversation with anyone and everyone. Standing on the corner and attracting attention came extremely easy for him. He was talkative, outgoing and very comfortable being around lots of people – just as he is today! These qualities were God-given, and they certainly benefited him in his life's calling to preach the Gospel.

Chapter 2

Salvation at Seventeen

(9) That if thou shalt confess with thy mouth the Lord Jesus, and shalt believe in thy heart that God hath raised him from the dead, thou shalt be saved.

Romans 10:9 KJV

The Petit family was relocated again. This time they moved to Tiffin, Ohio. There was a small Nazarene Church at 34 Oil Street. Charles and his brother Larry attended that church quite often, but they told their father that they were going to the movies on Sunday. After all, they had been raised Catholic and confirmed Lutheran.

Even so, it was the Pilgrim Holiness Church that Sister Grace Irvin had introduced them to as small children that fascinated Charles more than the Catholic Church or the Lutheran Church. And, this Nazarene Church was much like the Pilgrim Holiness Church.

There was also a cute little dark-haired, blue-eyed girl in the congregation who caught Charles's eye. She was later to become the mother of his nine children – six daughters and three sons.

In the Nazarene Church at 34 Oil Street, Charles found excitement. The people were enthusiastic in their singing, shouting and praising the Lord. This was the kind of church that he wanted to become a part of. These people were fun to be around and served the Lord with energy and exuberance. This was his kind of church.

At age seventeen (17), Charles received Jesus into his heart as his own personal Lord and Savior. He often jokes about his experience at the altar. He said that some people slapped him on the back and yelled, "Hold on!" Others slapped him on the back and yelled, "Let go!" Somewhere in between holding on and letting go, he got saved and received Christ into his life.

After receiving Christ into his life, the "calling" to preach the Gospel became even more apparent to him.

At age eighteen (18), Charles served in the Air Force (and very briefly in the Korean Conflict). Several years passed, and he married the cute little girl who had caught his eye in the Nazarene Church at 34 Oil Street.

While in Tiffin, Charles became a skilled glass blower, following in the footsteps of his father. In 1948, he was the youngest skilled glass blower in the United States. When he was a child in Ohio, West Virginia and Pennsylvania, he went to work with his dad and watched him blow glass, and he learned the trade from his dad.

Later on, Charles went to work for General Electric as a tool and die maker apprentice. As a tradesman, he became a millwright. Eventually, he worked his way into the engineering department where air craft engines were built. He retired from General Electric in 1993.

He worked for General Electric for a total of twenty-five (25) years, but they were not consecutive years, because when he pastored, he was usually a full time pastor. He pastored nearly forty-three (43) years.

Chapter 3

Built First New Church – Tiffin, Ohio

(11) And he gave some, apostles; and some, prophets; and some, evangelists; and some, pastors and teachers;
(12) For the perfecting of the saints, for the work of the ministry, for the edifying of the body of Christ.

Ephesians 4:11-12 KJV

Pastor Petit's first church was a storefront mission in Tiffin, Ohio. The building was a motorcycle shop located across the street from an A&P grocery store. On Saturday night, the motorcycles were moved from the showroom window to the back of the store so that Sunday morning services could be conducted.

The church smelled like motorcycle oil, but that did not hinder Pastor Petit. He wanted to have church, and where God guides, He provides. On Saturday afternoons, Pastor Petit stood in front of the A&P store and handed out flyers inviting people to the Pilgrim Holiness Mission across the street.

Twenty-one (21) year-old Pastor Petit and his congregation were in the storefront mission for about a year. Under his leadership, the mission thrived.

Seeing his potential as a leader, Pastor Charles Brubaker and Pastor Raymond Shafor encouraged him to pray about and consider building a new church. With that encouragement and the help of the Lord, Charles was on his way.

Pastor Petit found land on the outskirts of the city of Tiffin. He was twenty-one (21) years old and raring to go forward for the Lord, like a wild bronco that had just been released from the corral.

Not every church official was in favor of "that young Petit building a new church." They did not know that his first preaching engagement was with chickens in the chicken yard years ago. He had worked with the uninterested, the rebellious and the "doubters and pouters" long, long ago. He was now a seasoned pastor, according to himself.

The first new Pilgrim Holiness Church was built out of town and away from homes and businesses – an unlikely and undesirable place for some. But, when God is the Master Builder, success comes. The church now sits near the center of town, surrounded by many homes and businesses. It is a Pentecostal church, and it is doing well, fifty-eight (58) years later.

Pastor Charles J. Petit was destined to become a Pentecostal preacher. Ninety percent (90%) of the churches that Pastor Petit has built, pastored or been associated with are now Pentecostal churches.

Chapter 4

The Early 60's – Columbia, Mississippi

*(16) And he said, Come with me, and see my
zeal for the Lord...*

II Kings 10:16 KJV

Rev. Arnold Peck, Superintendent of the Gulf
State Home Missions, saw the zealous leadership
qualities in Pastor Petit, so he sent the Petit family to
Columbia, Mississippi, to pastor the Pilgrim Holiness
Church. They were promised a church, a congregation and a parsonage. So, Pastor Petit and his family,
which included five small girls, were off to Columbia,
Mississippi, in the early sixties (1960's) - a time of
social unrest in America, especially in the southern
states.

On the way to Mississippi, while traveling in the
fog, there was an accident. The Petit family car ran
into the back of a log truck and a log shot through the
windshield. By the mercy of God, no one was hurt.

Pastor Petit put a pillow in the damaged area and forged on, with the sweet little Petit girls in the back seat saying, "Are we there yet?"

When they arrived in Mississippi, they found a struggling church. Pastor Petit compensated his salary by selling Fuller Brush Products. That was right up his alley . . . he could be a "fisher of men" and a salesman at the same time. He invited everyone he met to the Pilgrim Holiness Church at 1210 Section Avenue (Park Avenue today).

The congregation grew, and the church flourished financially. Today, the church is a Pentecostal church with a day care, school and a nice parsonage.

While the Petit family lived in Mississippi, the first Petit son was born – Charles Samuel "Sam" Petit. The Petit family was so excited. It was a boy this time! Pastor Petit went back to church and announced, "Each little Petit girl has a brother!"

Someone from the congregation said, "You mean, Sister Petit had five boys?"

Sam grew into a fine young man. He served in Desert Storm and has two beautiful daughters and a lovely wife.

Pastor Petit was then called back to Ohio to pastor a church in Auburn, which is a rural farming area near Hamilton, Ohio. While pastoring in Auburn, he became acquainted with many good people who became friends for life. Many of these friends have gone on to be with the Lord.

After pastoring the Pilgrim Holiness Church in Auburn, he met Johnny Carter, a Pentecostal preacher full of fire and spunk. Johnny had the baptism of the Holy Ghost, speaking in other tongues as the Spirit gives utterance.

Pastor Petit was drawn to the Pentecostal movement. He knew what it was like to have "fire shut up in your bones" (Jeremiah 20:9). He had never been introduced to the gift of tongues as taught by the Pentecostal church, and he did not understand how the gifts could be manifested as they were among the Pentecostal rank. After traveling with Pastor Carter and other men of God and attending various Pentecostal churches, Pastor Petit received "the gift of speaking in tongues" (1 Corinthians 12:10).

Immediately, he was thrust into the Pentecostal movement. He did not want to bring confusion into the Nazarene/Pilgrim Holiness Church. But, he feared that if he denied this new "wonderful gift" that he had received, he would fail God. He longed to be pleasing to God, and he pursued more and more of the gifts of the Spirit with a passion and became a Pentecostal preacher.

Theresa Gray-Petit

Elect Rev. Petit Free Pentecostal Member Of Board

REV. PETIT

The Rev. Charles Petit, pastor of Pentecostal Church of God Tabernacle, 200 Belle Ave., was elected to the board of directors of the Free Pentecostal Church of God during a recently held convention in Cincinnati at the Free Pentecostal Church of God, 505 E. Liberty St., the Rev. Hobert B. Cole is pastor.

Many outstanding ministers from 16 different states attended this convention. Plans were formulated for a Pentecostal orphanage and camp ground area for the Miami Valley area.

The Rev. Mr. Petit has been affiliated with the Nazarene and Pilgrim Holiness Churches of this area. While pastoring in Tiffen, Ohio and Columbia, Miss., he pioneered new works for the Philgrim Holiness Church and served seven years on the Office Board of the Pilgrim Holiness Church.

He has been with the Free Pentecostal Church of Hamilton since November of 1966. Originally from Columbus, Ohio the Rev. Mr. Petit resides at 2005 Sparks Lane with his wife and their seven children, Cinda Sue, Ginger Rae, Carrie Jane, Shelly Rose, Theresa Mae, Samuel and John.

The first Pentecostal church that Pastor Petit pastored was Pater Avenue Pentecostal Church in Hamilton, Ohio. "Gobblers Knob" was what most people called that church. He pastored this church for six years and made many faithful friends. By the mercy and grace of God, and through much opposition and trials of his faith, Pastor Petit became a successful Pentecostal preacher.

According to historical documentation, Pater Avenue Pentecostal Church is the oldest Pentecostal church in Ohio.

While pastoring Pater Avenue Pentecostal Church, Pastor Petit became a member of the Free Pentecostal Church, Cincinnati headquarters, serving as a board member under the leadership of Bro. John Marcum.

Belle Avenue Pentecostal Church of God Tabernacle, 200 Belle Avenue, Hamilton, Ohio, was

The Free Pentecostal Church of God

Gobblers Knob
1321 Pater Avenue

Services Tuesday, 7:30 P.M. — Young People
Wed. 7:30 P.M. — Mid-Week Prayer and Praise
Saturday Night 7:30 P.M.
Sunday School — 10:00 A.M.
Sunday Evangelistic Service — 7:00 P.M.
Sunday Broadcast WMOH — 11:30 A.M.-12:00
WCNW Monday thru Friday — 1:00-1:15 P.M.

Rev. Charles Petit
3646 Hamilton-Mason Rd.
Hamilton, Ohio
Phone 892-5596

Pastor Petit's next church to pastor. The ministry thrived. The church was packed out in attendance every church night. There was a church choir, and there was a group of young teen girls who sang and called themselves "The Belle Tones." There was also a group of young teen boys called "The Originators." There was a church bus that the congregation used to take many trips to visit other churches for youth rallies and to go where Pastor Petit was a guest speaker. There was also a remodeling program going on through the direction of Pastor Petit. He was certainly a church builder and "mover and shaker" in the Pentecostal realm.

Sunday School attendance was growing by leaps and bounds under the direction of a young ambitious

Sunday School superintendent named Delbert Gray. The church had babies, children, teenagers, young married couples, middle aged and elderly parishioners. Everything was going well, and they were a happy, busy and grateful church under the leadership of Pastor Petit.

Pastor Petit had many friends, but the enemy is out to destroy that which God builds.

Pastor Petit and Congregation, Easter Sunday (1964)
There was always a lot of young people.
Pastor is in the lower right hand corner tending to
Sam, his oldest son born in Columbia, Mississippi.

The Petit Children
Left to right standing: Ginger Puckett, John Petit, Shelly
Smith, Dustin Petit, Sam Petit, Crystal Dickhaus
Left to right front row kneeling: Carrie
Jane Petit, Tessi Lee, Cinda Oser

Chapter 5

The Dark Years

(14) But every man is tempted, when he is drawn away of his own lust, and enticed.
(15) Then when lust hath conceived, it bringeth forth sin: and sin, when it is finished, bringeth forth death.

James 1:14-15 KJV

During the early seventies (70's), while pastoring and remodeling Belle Avenue Pentecostal Church of God Tabernacle, the pressures were many and great. To Pastor Petit, there seemed to be little time to study the Word, meditate or get alone with God to pray for guidance and direction.

Finances were such that Pastor Petit had to get an extra job to support his family. He worked 8 to 10 hours a day, preached out of town almost every night and tried to conduct his pastoral duties, and he just became overwhelmed with life as a pastor. He felt as if he had failed to be the pastor that God had called him to be.

We fail when we take our eyes off Jesus and put our eyes on our circumstances in life. There seemed to be so little time to devote to his wife and family.

During the early years, when Bro. Petit was studying for the ministry, he was mentored by Professor Charles Brubaker. The young men were warned of the pitfalls and snares set by the enemy that would await them in their ministry. Professor Brubaker told them that two of the biggest traps that the devil would lay for them would be the "love of money" and the "smell of perfume." Beware, keep your eyes on Jesus and your feet on the floor – lest you fall prey to the traps set before you.

Only through Christ can one endure the hardships that face us in life, and only through Christ can we truly embrace the spiritual benefits that are available for us such as: peace, comfort, joy, perseverance and the God-given grace to resist temptation.

Pastor Petit felt that if he could just get his family to Texas, he could make a fresh new beginning for himself and his family. But, that did not happen.

If you try to reform on your own, you only make things worse for yourself. Unrepented sin follows you wherever you go. Pastor Petit took his eyes "off Jesus" and had to pay severe consequences.

As the old saying goes, "Sin will take you farther

than you want to go, keep you longer than you want to stay, and cost you more than you want to pay." A dear friend of Pastor Petit's named Bill Slagle was the first one that I heard quote this saying.

Pastor Bill Slagle pastored in Metamora, Indiana, and has since gone home to be with Jesus. He was a powerful man of God, and he was a major support to Bro. Petit when the dark years ended and Bro. Petit started to reestablish his life as a "man of God."

Not everyone is in favor of the prodigal son returning home – not even his brother, as the scripture teaches. But, Pastor Slagle loved Bro. Petit and was a strong force in helping to place him back into the ministry. Pastor Slagle welcomed him home with open arms, allowed him to preach in his pulpit, prayed with Bro. Petit and gave him wise counseling.

Chapter 6

Eighty and Counting!

(15) He shall call upon me and I will answer him: I will be with him in trouble; I will deliver him and honour him.
(16) With long life will I satisfy him, and shew him my salvation.

Psalm 91:15-16 KJV

God has blessed Pastor Petit with long life and supernatural energy, far above any other eighty (80) year old that I know. When we get home after traveling fifteen (15) hours, he will carry in the luggage, go into the shed and get the lawnmower and cut the grass, wash the car, and then come into the house, pick up the phone and call about ten (10) people and tell them that he loves them, has been praying for them and hopes to see them in church on Sunday.... and that's one of his slow days. He can out work most fifty (50) year old men that I know. He redeems his time well, and I have never seen him waste God's money.

During Bro. Petit's years away from God, his young son, John, traveled with him and lived with him most of that time. Many times, Bro. Petit would lay by John, holding him tightly, fearing that Jesus may return before morning. He knew that if Jesus returned, John would be taken, and if he was holding on to his child, maybe Jesus would have mercy on him and take him too.

Bro. Petit knew that his lifestyle was not pleasing to God, but he never lost his fear of God or his belief in God. He missed the fellowship of the saints and longed for the return of the Spirit of the Lord in his life. He felt that he had drifted too far from shore and was doomed to be lost.

John would sit by his dad on the couch and put his arm around his dad's shoulders and pat him on the back and say, "Daddy, everything is going to be alright. It'll be ok." John became the parent, and his dad became the child. John experienced role reversal at a very young age.

During those dark years, while John was with his dad, he witnessed first-hand what sin and chaos can do to someone's life. John was in the adult world of construction workers where he was taken from state to state and from one job location to another. He learned to operate heavy equipment and pushed coal barges down the Mississippi River by age twelve (12).

Later in life, John became a very successful businessman, building salt domes throughout the United States. One day, I asked John if those domes were hard to build. He said, "Oh no. It's easy . . . just like putting a puzzle together."

Pastor Petit was living with Carrie, his daughter, when tragedy struck the Petit family. He had been back with the Lord for several years and had gotten back into pastoring. A knock came on his bedroom door around three o'clock in the morning. It was Carrie, "Dad, John had a truck accident in Wichita Falls, Kansas."

Pastor Petit jumped up, quickly grabbed his pants and jumped into them and said, "I'll go to him!"

Carrie replied, "Dad, it is too late. John's gone."

That became the darkest day in Pastor Petit's life. John and his crew of men went over a sixty-five (65) foot embankment in the state of Kansas. John did not survive. He was twenty-eight (28) years old and had been married just a little over one year. He and his crew had been building a salt dome in that area of the United States. The accident happened on Father's Day and his mother's birthday.

Thank God that Pastor Petit had been back with the Lord during this time. Only God's mercy and the love of his family could sustain him and carry him through such a tragedy.

The Petit family is a remarkably amazing group of people. They came together, loved and supported one another and made it through. Sam, John's older brother, said, "John always had to be first."

One never gets over the death of a child. You just learn to live with it, only by the grace and mercy of God. That's not the proper order of things – our children are supposed to outlive us.

John was tall and handsome, and he had brilliantly white teeth and a smile that could melt your heart. He was a very hard worker (as all the Petit's are), and he had a heart of gold and a generous and forgiving spirit. He now waits in Heaven for his family . . . and what a marvelous family that is!

Chapter 7

The Prodigal Son

*(21) And the son said unto him, Father, I have
sinned against heaven and in thy sight, and am
no more worthy to be called thy son.*

*(22) But the father said to his servants, Bring
forth the best robe, and put it on him; and put
a ring on his hand, and shoes on his feet:*

*(23) And bring hither the fatted calf, and kill it;
and let us eat, and be merry;*

*(24) For this my son was dead, and is alive
again; he was lost, and is found. And they
began to be merry."*

Luke 15:21-24 KJV

Pastor Petit blamed no one for his backslidden condition, except himself. The enemy would have us point fingers of blame at others to justify our actions. It is easier to see the faults in others than to see the faults within ourselves. Remember, scripture teaches us that we are drawn away by our own lusts. When we take our eyes off Jesus, we can be drawn into sin and chaos.

During his backslidden years, Bro. Petit carried his Bible with him. He placed it right beside him on the front seat of his car. His construction buddies and friends noticed his Bible. Many of them asked him why he carried that Bible with him wherever he went, knowing the lifestyle he was living. He would always tell them, "That is my road map back home."

It was a long, heartbreaking, treacherous, uphill battle for him that lasted 16½ years before he finally made it "back home."

When the prodigal son came to himself and realized just how far he had descended into sin, he went home. His father did not say, "What are you doing here?" or "I told you so." His father welcomed him with open arms, gave him the family ring, the finest robe and prepared a huge feast for him (Luke 15:21-24).

Our Heavenly Father welcomes us back into the family, holds nothing against us and washes us clean, just as if we have never sinned.

Oft' times it is hard for our brothers and sisters to forgive us because we have disappointed or hurt them. They have not forgotten the pain that we caused them through our disobedience to God.

We are not righteous, but through Christ we can find righteousness. Our righteousness is His righteousness through us. No man is righteous.

The enemy will tell those in a backslidden condition that they have gone too far to turn back, and that no one will ever have confidence in them again. That may partially be true, but the enemy mixes truth and lies together to cause us to believe a lie and be lost. I like to say, "For every one person who doesn't have confidence in a child of God returning home, five hundred (500) will have confidence in him/her." With God on your side, who's going to win? You are!

So, if you are in a backslidden condition today, go back home. Your Heavenly Father is waiting with the ring, the robe and the fatted calf (spiritually speaking). If you preached, preach again! If you sang, sing again! If you were a teacher, teach again! If you raised your hands to God and danced in the Spirit, dance again!

It is not too late for you to return home and reestablish your life in Christ. God will cleanse you as white as snow, set your feet on the straight and narrow path, and guide you in the right direction.

In 1992, Bro. Petit came into Belle Avenue Pentecostal Church where Pastor Saul Davidson was pastor. That was the church that Bro. Petit had walked away from 16½ years earlier.

Pastor Davidson, who really did not know Bro. Petit, had been praying for him for eleven (11) years. Many people loved Bro. Petit and prayed for him during those dark years while he was away from his calling.

When Bro. Petit stepped forward and knelt at the altar, the men of God came forward, formed a protective hedge around him and helped him to pray his way back home. The three men that stand out in my mind were Glenn Price, Elmer Howard and Clint Davidson. I know there were others, and God knows all the people who supported, encouraged and accepted Bro. Petit back into the family of God. God keeps an account of everything. Pastor Saul Davidson and the congregation were instrumental in helping Bro. Petit to become reestablished in his calling.

I must not forget Sister Gertrude Roberson, who pastors a church in Williamsdale, Ohio. She had a television program, and she invited Bro. Petit to preach on the program.

That was it! The exposure on the television program became his launching pad back into the ministry. He received calls to come and preach from pastors who knew him years ago, and the calls have never stopped coming in, "Bro. Petit, can we count on you to preach here and to preach there?"

Thank you, God, and thank you, Pastor Gertrude Roberson.

Pastor Petit prays for all young men and women who have the desire to go into the ministry. The enemy works overtime, often coming as an angel of light, to entice them away. Beware of the pitfalls that await you. Stay focused on your "calling," and stay faithful to Jesus. Keep yourself in good company and receive sound doctrine and constructive counseling.

Trust in the Lord with all your heart and lean not unto your own understanding; in all your ways, acknowledge the Lord, and He will direct your paths (Proverbs 3:5-6). For the Lord will be your confidence and will keep your foot established on the Rock.

Young ministers, establish your feet in Christ. Become rooted and grounded in the Word of God, to the point that when the storms rage and the winds blow, you will not be uprooted and destroyed. There is a place in Jesus where that is possible. Jesus is your fortress, your refuge and your tower of strength. Dwell therein!

Chapter 8

New Beginning Tabernacle

(18) And I say also unto thee, That thou art Peter, and upon this rock I will build my church; and the gates of hell shall not prevail against it.

Matthew 16:18 KJV

After Pastor Petit came back home to the family of God, he was amazed by the outpouring of love and acceptance that he received from his brothers and sisters in the Lord. Many people had prayed for his return during those dark years of his life. He was so thankful to God, and was determined to serve the Lord, come what may, for the rest of his days. He had no intentions of pastoring again, but he did want to be obedient to the Spirit of the Lord.

So, he told God, "Do with me as You please. I will go where You send me." He was glad to be back under the shadow of the cross and in the arms of Jesus. He was almost sixty (60) years old, and it was in God's plans for Pastor Petit to build a new church at age seventy (70) – that was to come later.

While working under the leadership of Pastor Saul Davidson, Bro. Petit felt the "call" from God to pastor again. Remember, he did tell God that he would go wherever God wanted him to go. He located a small vacant church in the inner city of Hamilton, Ohio, and the rest is history. The rush was on – there was no holding him back now!

We named the new church New Beginning Tabernacle because Bro. Petit had certainly been given a "new beginning" in his life. With the blessings of Pastor Saul Davidson, and the Lord, Bro. Petit was on his way to becoming Pastor Petit again!

Charlie Farthing and a few other men came to clear the land around the church and prepare the area for parking. Others came to clean and decorate the church in preparation for services.

On opening day, the church was filled to capacity. The guest speaker was Bro. C.B. Ellis, the former General Overseer of the Mountain Assembly Church of God. He was a dear and faithful friend of Pastor Petit's. He had prayed for him for many years and encouraged him to turn his life back to God.

Charlie Farthing, A Faithful Friend

Left to right: Pastor Charles Petit,
Arlo Barger, Rev. C.B. Ellis

People came and helped us, and Pastor Petit's ministry was reestablished - alive and well! We were at 400 S. Front Street for two and one half (2½) years, and the congregation grew so large that we had to find a bigger church.

The congregation at New Beginning Tabernacle moved to a larger church at 199 Highland Avenue in New Miami, Ohio. We, with the help of God, outgrew that building and needed a bigger parking lot within about three years.

The next destination for the congregation of New Beginning Tabernacle was 2551 Ramona Lane in Fairfield, Ohio. There, we had land and room to expand. It was a pastor's dream. That is where the Lord bid Pastor Petit to build a new sanctuary.

Build a new church? He was nearly seventy (70) years old. His first church was built when he was twenty-two (22). Wasn't that too young? Now, at seventy (70), he's building a new church. Isn't that too old? No, not in God's eyes!

The congregation purchased a building that was being used as a warehouse. The building was a former chicken house that had been converted into a church by Pastors Bobby and Faye Grove, years earlier.

Pastor Bobby had to sell the church to a man that was now using it to store building materials. God had a plan and purpose for that building. Pastor Petit was the man chosen by God to pick up the vision of Bobby and Faye Grove and run with it.

Pastor Petit has the tenacity of a bull dog. When he lays hold on a project, he won't let go. He holds tight and firm and rushes forward, full speed, to get the job done.

New Beginning Tabernacle "Ground Breaking Day"
Left to right: Roy Moore (Music Director/
Trustee), Theresa Petit,
Pastor Charles Petit
Board Members and Trustees:
Paul Gibson, Cecil Combs, Phillip Grubb,
Challis Hodge, Martin Bowling, Ira Butler

John Fields breaking ground for the new church.
Pastor Petit giving directions with
board members looking on.

The list of people who came to our aid during the building of the new sanctuary is long and numerous. God sent people from the north, the south, the east and the west. Pastor Petit had a radio broadcast on WCNW in Fairfield every Saturday at noon! Truck drivers heard Pastor Petit tell the public about the new church that was being built in Fairfield, Ohio. They pulled off the interstate, came to the radio station and brought donations for the building fund.

Old friends, new friends, enemies and the like supported this work with their prayers and

finances. Pastor Petit found favor with the city offi-
cials, local business people from Hyde's Restaurant,
Ron's Car Wash, Brown-Dawson Funeral Home,
Colligans Funeral Home, Mill's Moving & Storage,
M&M Car Sales, Dustin Petit's Carpet Installation,
Carroll's Carpet Installation, Barnes Electric and
Cliff Richardson's Painting Service. There were so
many others that supported the New Beginning
Tabernacle that it would take a very thick book to
list them all.

Local pastors, like Thurman and Irene McIntosh,
bought the chandeliers and carpet for the church. I
cannot remember everyone, but God does.

Arlo and Imogene Barger were true friends of ours,
and we are grateful for every prayer and every act of
kindness. No act of kindness was wasted.

Pastor Petit also found favor with First Financial
Bank, and most important of all, he found favor with
God – the Master Builder.

The original chicken house part of the church
became the fellowship hall, the offices and the edu-
cational wing for Sunday School. A new and very
beautiful sanctuary with huge oak laminated arches
was built, thanks to our many friends and supporters,
and especially our thanks to God for His divine grace
and guidance.

Pastor Petit "on the job," giving instructions.

Footer for New Beginning Tabernacle

Laminated Arches

Laminated Arches for the New Church

Time for Brick!
Brick for the old chicken house and new sanctuary.

New Beginning Tabernacle Board Members/Trustees
Left to right: Tony Stubbs, Pastor Charles Petit,
Phillip Grubb, Cecil Combs, Challis Hodge,
Paul Gibson, Ira Butler, Martin Bowling

If God has called you to do a work, He will provide for you. God will give you supernatural energy and a peace that you are not able to understand. He will give you the ability to love the unlovable. God will give you perseverance and determination to finish what you started for Him. Don't give up, forge forward and keep your eye on the prize! Faint not. Your strength comes from the Lord. He will never let you down. He will place people in your life to help you accomplish the task set before you.

We pastored New Beginning Tabernacle seventeen (17) years. Pastor Petit has stepped down from pastoring, but he is going full force in the ministry, in the evangelistic field.

Pastor Petit fills in for Pastor Bryan Walton at Placida Road Church of God in Grove City, Florida, when he needs him. Pastor Bryan and Elsie Walton are dear and precious friends of ours. We also travel throughout the United States preaching, ministering and working for the Lord.

My life with Pastor Petit is full and rich with the abundant blessings of God. We have a common goal in life, and that goal is to lead others to Christ.

New Beginning Tabernacle is now pastored by Pastors Bobby and Faye Grove. The Lord has placed them back into a work that was started by them many years ago. The church is called Soul Winners Church, and soul winners they certainly are. Soul Winners Church is thriving and doing well.

Chapter 9

A Tribute to Our Friends

(24) A man that hath friends must shew him-self friendly: and there is a friend that sticketh closer than a brother.

Proverbs 18:24 KJV

Pastor Petit and I certainly do appreciate the prayers, love and support of our many faithful friends that have worked along beside us during our years of pastoring, and our years of ministry, in general. The churches that were built; the souls that were saved; the foreign missionary trips; and, the many miles travelled were the direct result of the prayers and support of our friends and family.

First and foremost, God has blessed us with good health, sound minds, guts, perseverance and tolerance to endure the hardships and embrace the pleasures of working in the ministry. We honor God and glorify Him as our Lord and Savior and our Provider and Guide.

Without Christ, all is in vain. With Christ, ". . . all things work together for good to them that love God . . . and are called according to His purpose" (Romans 8:28 KJV). We can do all things which Jesus Christ guides and directs us to do (Philippians 4:13).

There are friends who are faithful forever, and there are those who are faithful only for a season, sometimes for a short season. "To everything there is a season, and a time to every purpose under the heaven" (Ecclesiastes 3:1 KJV).

When I think about our most precious friends, I often think of Tom Napier from Hamilton, Ohio. Tom came to Pastor Petit's ministry when he was a teenager. He carried bricks during the remodeling of Belle Avenue Pentecostal Church of God Tabernacle. Tom worked diligently during the remodeling of that church.

Tom has a signature song that he sings when he is attending church. That song is "Working On A Building." Tom has kept in touch with Pastor Petit for over fifty (50) years. He calls us on our anniversary, and he never forgets my birthday. He calls us when he feels that we need to know news from home (Ohio).

Tom, we love you and we want to spend eternity with you in Heaven. God bless you, Tom. You have a big heart and a precious soul.

If we could hand out trophies, rewards and blue ribbons to our many friends, we would, but that is not possible.

Someday, we shall receive our reward. "For the Son of man shall come in the glory of his Father with his angels; and then He shall reward every man according to his works" (Matthew 16:27 KJV).

Like the old saying says:

> Life is like a journey
> taken on a train,
> With a pair of travelers
> at each window pane.
> I may sit beside you
> all the journey through,
> Or I may sit elsewhere,
> never knowing you.
> If God should place me
> by your side,
> Let's be pleasant travelers –
> it is such a short ride.

Jesus tells us to love one another as He loved us. That is actually a commandment (John 13:34). "Greater love hath no man than this, that a man lay down his life for his friends" (John 15:13 KJV).

Laying down your life for a friend can be as simple

as sacrificing your time to be with a friend in need, visiting a friend when he's in the hospital or when he misses church. Take time out of your busy day to call someone on the phone who needs to be encouraged. Take that person out to lunch that is ignored by everyone else. Show yourself friendly. Treat your enemies as friends. Jesus called Judas a friend.

Jesus didn't ask us to die on a cross, but he did command us to love one another as He loved us.

Make new friends
And keep the old,
Some are silver,
And some are gold.

KENTUCKY

COLONELS

In Loving Memory of Lifelong Friends and Supporters
Pastor Ray Anderson (Cincinnati, Ohio)
J.D. Jarvis, Musician and Songwriter (Hamilton, Ohio)

New Miami pastor takes message to Asia

By Peggy McCracken
Journal-News

NEW MIAMI

Petit

While most of Butler County slept last Sunday morning, across the world in Manila, the Philippines, Pastor Charles Petit of New Miami's New Beginning Tabernacle was busy stirring the hearts of the faithful.

"When it's two in the afternoon there, it's two in the morning here," said Petit before his trip. "I told them (his congregation) to set their clocks to five till two and start praying for us."

Petit and his wife, Theresa, were special guests at the 19th church anniversary of the Federation of Churches in Manila. Invited by the Rev. Rey G. Manulid, president of Living Hope Christian Bible College-Marantha Living Hope Academy in the Philippines, the Petits planned to visit 17 churches during their weeklong stay.

Manulid contacted Petit in July and invited him to serve as the anniversary service speaker. Although Petit has preached and pastored through the United States, this was his first trip aboard.

Petit, who does not speak Spanish, was to speak through an interpreter. His host advised him he'd have to speak a little slower than usual when preaching.

"I get excited about the Gospel," he said.

The theme of the gathering was "Praise the Lord," based on Matthew 28:19-20. Although Petit was preparing his sermon on that scripture, he acknowledged that when the Holy Spirit takes over a service, anything goes.

The doors have simply opened since Petit and his wife received the invitation.

"I certainly appreciate the community and the churches who have made it possible for us to go," said Petit, who received financial support from his church as well as Glory Road Baptist Church, Lighthouse Tabernacle in Metamora, Ind., a church in Loveland and several business people.

Turning 65 in October — "I tell them I'm 64 plus change" — Petit said he has "pioneered" several churches in the area, including Auburn Pilgrim Holiness Church and Belle Avenue Pentecostal Church in 1969.

The Tiffin native left the ministry for a few years but felt called to return to the pulpit full time. He started the New Miami church less than five years ago and has watched the membership grow to 200.

Pastor Rey Manulid's Church (Philippines, 1998)
We (Pastor and Sis. Petit) are praying for the people.

Pastor Rey Manulid and Pastor Petit praying for
people at a cell church in the Philippines.

Marantha Living Hope Academy (Elementary Bible School)
Santa Rose, Philippines (1998)

Missionary Trip To Santa Rosa, Philippines (1998)

Theresa Gray-Petit

IN THE SPIRIT

Fairfield pastor works with Manila church

Petit visiting group during anniversary

BY PEGGY MCCRACKEN
JOURNALNEWS

FAIRFIELD — Some people have friends in high places. Some in far places.

The Rev. Charles Petit is one of the latter.

He's been away the past week visiting the friends he made years ago in the Philippines. The Tiffin native is taking time from his duties as pastor of the New Beginning Tabernacle on Ramona Lane in Fairfield to work with the Federation of Churches in Manila.

Petit, 74, was invited as a guest for the federation's 26th anniversary, returning to the area after a seven-year absence. He anticipated visiting the organization's 17 churches, the Bible college Marantha Living Hope Academy and its nursing home.

"My main purpose is to preach 'Every believer a Christ disciple and every disciple a Christian leader,'" said Petit.

His visit with the Rev. Rey

Rev. Charles Petit

G. Manulid, president of the academy, will include efforts to help organize the area pastors.

"We want to get the pastors together at least once a month," he said of the pastors who are often without support of fellow ministers. "Where there is unity, there is strength."

While not related to the local pastor, Michael Charles Petit of the Free Gospel Bible Institute will be working with Petit and Manulid in the Philippines.

In the past 10 years, the Fairfield pastor has spoken at 65 conventions, had more than 500 preaching engagements and has assisted with eight new churches. He has pastored many years in the area and started New Beginning Tabernacle in New Miami in the mid-1990s.

Contact **Peggy McCracken** at (513) 820-2169, or e-mail her at pmccracken@coxohio.com.

Missionary Trip to the Philippines (2005)

64

Pastor Petit Preaching in the Philippines (2005)

Dennis Madriz and Pastor Petit (Philippines, 2005)
Dennis was an evangelist working out of
the New Beginning Tabernacle.
Dennis is pastoring a church in the Cincinnati, Ohio area.

Chapter 10

Growing As a Christian

(20) . . . And, lo, I am with you always, even unto the end of the world.

Matthew 28:20 KJV

Growing as a Christian is a great adventure. One must be disciplined, committed and persistent. Apostle Paul explains it in Ephesians 3:16-19 KJV:

(16) That he would grant you, according to the riches of his glory, to be strengthened with might by his Spirit in the inner man;

(17) That Christ may dwell in your hearts by faith; that ye, being rooted and grounded in love,

(18) May be able to comprehend with all saints what is the breadth, and length, and depth, and height;

(19) And to know the love of Christ, which

passeth knowledge, that ye might be filled
with all the fullness of God.

I believe in the power of prayer and positive speaking in one's life. The tongue is a little member, but a great fire can result from a very small flame. The tongue, no man can tame. It is unruly, evil and full of poison, according to the scripture.

God gives mercy and grace to us, as it is only through Christ that we can live a clean life, resist the devil and bridle our tongue. A wise person who has God-given knowledge has good conversation and meekness of wisdom. We are to keep our tongue from speaking evil.

Sin can be compared to cancer of the soul:

- Offense becomes hurt.
- Hurt becomes bitterness.
- Bitterness becomes hate.

When hate is conceived, it has roots that reach deep into the heart and spiritual death results. Hate poisons the soul.

The only remedy for spiritual death is the Spirit of the Lord. The Spirit of the Lord can reach way down deep into the heart and pull out the embedded roots of sin and destroy them.

God forgives us and chooses to forget our sins. We

must learn to forgive ourselves and those who have offended and hurt us.

Do not get on the hurt train. It is the same as the sin train. It will take you farther than you want to go, keep you longer than you want to stay and cost you more than you want to pay. I've known people who have been out of church for years because they allowed one person to hurt them. Do not fall for that familiar trick of the enemy. The scripture tells us that we cannot go through life without becoming offended. Deal with hurt right away. Do not cut off your destiny in Christ by holding on to hurt.

You are wonderfully and marvelously made to serve the Lord, and it is your responsibility as a Christian to love and forgive those who have caused you pain, just as Jesus forgave us!

So, if you want to grow as a Christian, do not allow others to stunt your growth. Seek the Lord with all your heart. He will give you power and strength to overcome. He will give you "keeping power."

As Christians, we should strive to be like Jesus as much as we possibly can by our actions and our words. Sharing one's faith with others is just a natural result from loving God and wanting to please our Heavenly Father.

A seasoned Christian is one who has "seen it all"

– the committed, the compassionate and the compromisers. I prefer to be committed and compassionate. When you compromise with sin, you are exposing yourself to disgrace and dishonor. Be strong in the Lord. Know who you are in Christ. Abide in Christ and allow Him to abide in you. Satan trembles at the name of Jesus. Jesus will be your best friend if you will allow Him to be. Jesus loves you.

Chapter 11

Retirement! What Retirement?

Pastor Petit's Badge of Honor

(4) I must work the works of him that sent me, while it is day: the night cometh, when no man can work.

John 9:4 KJV

Retirement does not exist for those whose lives are dedicated to the building up of the Kingdom of God. Our duties may change; our position in life may change; our geographical location may change, but our minds and hearts are working diligently to win more souls.

Since Pastor Petit stepped down from pastoring, we have more time to work in the evangelistic field. We are also involved with helping local churches in our hometown in Florida. When your soul burns within you to work for the Lord, that's what you have to do.

Even though Pastor Petit is nearly eighty (80) years old, age has not overtaken him. Years ago, when he was in his early seventies (70's), the teens in church gave him a huge pin-on button that says, "I'm not old, I'm a Recycled Teenager!" And, that is exactly what he is!

He had prostate cancer in 2011. God brought him through surgery in a miraculous way. He had a wonderful doctor, Dr. Robert Carey in Sarasota, Florida. Dr. Carey believes in the healing power of God, and he is not ashamed to join hands and pray before surgery.

Some call retirement "stepping down." Some call it "stepping up." I call it "entering into a new season of one's life." Ecclesiastes 3:1 KJV says, "To every thing there is a season, and a time to every purpose under the heaven."

Ecclesiastes 12:13 KJV tells us to ". . . Fear God, and keep his commandments: for this is the whole duty of man."

If we wait upon the Lord, He will renew our strength; we shall run and not be weary; and, walk and not faint (Isaiah 40:31).

We have a wonderful friend and brother in the Lord who pastors in Hudson, North Carolina. His name is Pastor Fred Stapleton. Every November, around Thanksgiving, Pastor Petit preaches to the teenagers in Pastor Fred's church. Those young people have been taught to greatly respect the elderly. They are attentive, accommodating and very considerate.

Pastor Fred is a great role model for the young Christian. He has traveled to many countries in the missionary field, and the young people have also been on the mission field along with him. We appreciate Pastor Fred and Connie, their family and their church.

I would like to give recognition to a few pastors and their wives that we hold dear to our hearts:

- Pastor Walt and Michelle Sparks – Bloomingdale, Georgia (near Savannah)
- Pastor Curtis and Daintry Manning – Sevierville, Tennessee
- Pastor J.R and Patty Robbins – Kings Mountain, North Carolina
- Pastor Brady and Teresa Jackson – Kings Mountain, North Carolina

- Pastor Rick and Kelli Badgerow – Port Charlotte, Florida
- Pastor Bryan and Elsie Walton – Grove City, Florida
- Pastor Welton and Anna Lane – Louisville, Kentucky
- Pastor Claude and Phyllis Franklin – Indianapolis, Indiana
- Pastor Jay and Kara Lynne Brubaker – St. Petersburg, Florida
- Pastor Elizabeth Hoskins – Laurel, Indiana

There are so many more. God knows them all. These men and women have dedicated their time, energy, resources and their very lives to their calling.

"And how shall they preach, except they be sent? As it is written, How beautiful are the feet of them that preach the gospel of peace, and bring glad tidings of good things!" Romans 10:15 KJV.

Also, a special "Thank you" goes to Rick and Brenda Sparks, Harold and Carla Porterfield, and Alex of Bloomingdale, Georgia.

Retirement does not mean to cease from living. Retirement is a "new beginning" and can be the best season of your life. It can be a time of enrichment, and a time of "having time to spend with your family." Stay busy, be active and witness for the Lord, either by the words you speak or by the life you live in front of others. Take time to listen to people, not with just your ears but listen with your heart. Tell others about the mercy, peace and love that can only come from serving God.

Retirement is a time to make new friends and value and be thankful for the ones you already have. Do not forget where you came from, and do not forget those who helped you get to where you are today.

Chapter 12

Eat the Watermelon . . .
Spit Out the Seeds

(8) Finally, brethren, whatsoever things are true, whatsoever things are honest, whatsoever things are just, whatsoever things are pure, whatsoever things are lovely, whatsoever things are of good report;. . .think on these things.

Philippians 4:8 KJV

Life is full of decisions - some are simple, and some are difficult. The decisions that we make in life can determine our destiny. Wrong decisions can result in failure and disappointments. Right decisions can bring success and happiness.

It is within our power to eat the watermelon and spit out the seeds that will cause harm to our body, mind, spirit and soul. Seeds of doubt, hurt, bitterness, criticism, hate and revenge can grow within our heart and can choke and destroy our spiritual connection with Jesus Christ, our Savior.

We must choose, with the help of the Spirit of the Lord, to eat the sweet tasting watermelon of the Word, and spit out the seeds that would be harmful to our victorious walk with Jesus.

The sweet fruit of the watermelon can be compared to the sweet fruit of the Spirit – love, joy, peace, long suffering, gentleness, goodness, faith, meekness and temperance (Galatians 5:22-23). For the fruit of the spirit is in all goodness, righteousness and truth. We are to have no fellowship with the unfruitful works of darkness, but rather reprove them according to God's word.

We are to bear one another's burdens, and if we see our brother overtaken in a fault or sin, we are to restore him, not destroy him, in the spirit of meekness and forgiveness, lest we be tempted.

The scripture tells us in Proverbs 21:23 KJV, "Whoso keepeth his mouth, and his tongue keepeth his soul from troubles."

When you see your brother overtaken in a sinful situation, take it to the Lord in prayer. As we have the opportunity, let us do good unto all men. He that soweth good seed to the spirit shall reap life everlasting (Galatians 6:8).

Last Sunday, Pastor Rick Badgerow of Praise

Tabernacle in Port Charlotte, Florida, stated in his sermon, "When you are where God wants you to be, you are in 'the perfect place'." I started thinking about "the perfect place." Our physical bodies are the temple that God created for our soul and spirit to reside in; therefore, our bodies are a "perfect place" because they were created by God. It is our responsibility to be proud of, and to take care of, that which God has given us.

The "perfect place" spiritually is when we are centered on Jesus and the building up of the Kingdom of God. That should be our main goal in life as Christians.

God has a plan, purpose and destiny for each one of us. We are all the same, yet we are different. We have the same physical, emotional and spiritual needs. We all need to be loved and accepted.

We are born with an emptiness in our heart that can only be filled and satisfied by the Spirit of the Lord. It is our choice to accept Jesus into our hearts. We can allow Him to pilot our ship on this sea of life, which can often become rough and turbulent. The calming of that sea can only be achieved through our relationship with Jesus, and He will say, "Peace, be still," and, peace will come to us, only through Jesus (Mark 4:39).

Jesus died on the cross and shed His blood so that we could live life more abundantly here on earth.

Whenever we abandon this ship of life, we will take a "plain air ride" to Heaven where we will certainly find "The Perfect Place."

Pastor Petit and I have one ultimate goal in life. That goal is to lead others to the cross so that they can accept Jesus as their personal Savior and reap the benefits that Christ has for us when we EAT THE WATERMELON . . . AND SPIT OUT THE SEEDS!

Anna Rose and Alex McCloskey, Great-Grandchildren

Chapter 13

Everyone Has a Book Within!

I will praise thee; for I am fearfully and won-
derfully made: marvelous are thy works; and
that my soul knoweth right well.

Psalms 139:14 KJV

I recently purchased a Christmas card for my fabulous eleven (11) year-old granddaughter, Rayne. On the front of the card it read, "How are you like a snowflake?" On the inside, it said, "You are beautiful, you are one of a kind, and you were sent from Heaven above."

Each one of us is a gift from God, according to scripture. We were uniquely and beautifully created by God for His pleasure and purpose.

Each one of us is placed on the road of life – some have a longer journey than others. On the road of life, there are pitfalls and stumbling blocks placed there by the enemy. With the help of God, we can overcome every trap placed in our path. If we stumble, and even if we fall, God is there to pick us up, place us back on the path called "straight," and guide us in the right direction – over and over again. Isaiah 40:4 KJV says, "Every valley shall be exalted, and every mountain and hill shall be made low: and the crooked shall be made straight, and the rough places plain."

One of the simplest tasks in life is to write about one's own self. It could be a book or just a personal journal to pass down from one generation to the next. Wouldn't you cherish a book or journal written by your great-great-great grandmother about her life and place in history? Wouldn't you love to write about some of the pitfalls of life that you have encountered and been deceived by so that you can warn and advise your grandchildren about following the same path?

You could relate to your descendants and friends about how God has delivered you from the snares of Satan, has kept you safe and given you a sound mind and strong spirit to overcome your trials, tribulations and failures.

We all have a book within us. We contain unique and valuable information that we can pass along to the next generation. If you feel inspired to write a book or journal about your life, do so.

You are a valuable individual, and God loves you.

You were created to serve God and lead others to Christ. Through your writing, you may be able to fulfill your purpose on a grand scale.

You may have friends and loved ones who scoff at the idea, or you may have friends and loved ones who will encourage you and look forward to reading your finished work. You may have both audiences.

Autobiographies are probably the simplest books to create. Biographies are next in line. Writing about yourself or your dearest friends and/or your most precious loved ones can be an enlightening and amazing experience. Writing a book may bring out hidden emotions that need to be brought out, dealt with and conquered, especially when we are honest and straightforward about our life's experiences . . . failures and successes.

You never know where your book or journal may end up. Fifty (50) years after writing it, it may end up on a thrift store bookshelf, and then in the possession of an individual who may be going through what you went through and need spiritual guidance or help. God's word is the same yesterday, today and forever (Hebrews 13:8). The person picking up your book may find the encouragement needed to go on for another day, another week, another month or perhaps until Jesus comes.

As we all know, the greatest book ever written is the Bible. The Bible is our road map home.

Following the advice of Jesus is our greatest accomplishment. Jesus will be your very best Friend, if you will allow Him to be. He is a friend who sticks "closer than a brother" (Proverbs 18:24). He is our Savior, our Healer, our Provider, our Comforter and our Guide. When you turn your life over to Christ, you will never be the same. It is as simple as Romans 10:9-10 KJV:

> 9. That if thou shalt confess with thy mouth the Lord Jesus, and shalt believe in thine heart that God hath raised him from the dead, thou shalt be saved.
>
> 10. For with the heart man believeth unto righteousness; and with the mouth confession is made unto salvation.

Final Word

Pastor Petit and I pray that this book has strengthened your spiritual life and given you positive insight into your walk with God. If you have not accepted Jesus in your heart, today is the day of salvation. We hope to share Heaven with you some day!

Love & Prayers To All.

May God's Blessings Overtake You,
Theresa Gray-Petit

Special Acknowledgements

Melissa C. Knight, my editor, coordinator and faithful friend. Thank you for the many hours you sacrificed to help me to complete my first book.

Alex and Anna Rose McCloskey, our great grandchildren on the front cover. Thank you, Alex, for "not eating" all the watermelon during the photo shoot by Nana (Shelly Smith) and Mom (Shannon McCloskey).

Wes and Angie Scenters (Hamilton, Ohio) – "your friendship is priceless."

Jim and Shirley Wimmer (Hamilton, Ohio) – "dedicated workers for Christ."

Beverly Ion (London, Kentucky) – "faithful and dependable."

Lifelong Friends
Carolyn Sue "Shirley" Orr (Dayton, Ohio)

We have been side by side since Junior High School. Thank you for standing by my side during life's greatest tragedies. Thank you for making Mom laugh – not everyone could do that.

I appreciate you for being with Mom when the angels came to escort her to glory. I know that was not easy for you.

You have been blessed by God with the talent to sing, the gift of counsel and the ability to continue on through life's greatest challenges.

God has enriched my life by putting you by my side.

I must add – you're the greatest cook in the world. Your huge cat head biscuits melt in one's mouth even without butter!

You have the ability to cause people to laugh and laugh and laugh some more. That is a gift from God! We have laughed through some very tragic events in our lives (and cried too).

I love you. You have blessed my life abundantly.

Vicki Lynn Jarvis (Franklin, Ohio)

We have been friends since Elementary School.

The first time I saw you, your brother, Ricky Allen, was pulling you along our gravely, dusty, dirt road on an old door. He was using the door for a wagon. It seems like yesterday, but it has been almost fifty-five (55) years.

God blessed you to become a registered nurse. You have helped many, many people during your distinguished career. I call you an angel of mercy. You are an amazingly honest person.

Thank you for your faithfulness as my devoted friend and for your love and prayers for all these years.

Thank you for being there when I need you. I love you and, and you are always in my prayers.

About The Author

Theresa Gray-Petit was born and raised in Hamilton, Ohio (north of Cincinnati). She graduated from Garfield Senior High School in 1967. She married her high-school sweetheart, and they were married for twenty-five (25) years when she became a widow in 1992.

When her son was a senior in high school, she decided to attend college. Theresa graduated from Miami University in Oxford, Ohio, in 1995, and obtained a degree in Arts and Humanities with her studies that included: religion, sociology, biology, philosophy and creative writing.

She always had a strong desire to encourage others through her ability to write. Many church members have received a letter of encouragement from her. Those letters, she feels, have been inspired by God to bring hope and confidence to those who have been beaten down by the cares of life.

Writing "Eat The Watermelon . . . Spit Out The Seeds" is an attempt to show others that God is loving, merciful and forgiving. We are all human and subject to failure when we take our eyes off Jesus.

Theresa and her husband, Charles J. Petit, pastored the New Beginning Tabernacle in Fairfield, Ohio, for seventeen (17) years. They are retired from pastoring, but not from the ministry. They travel throughout the United States, evangelizing and teaching the Word of God. They currently reside in Port Charlotte, Florida, with their two dogs, Snuggles and Tootsie.

Theresa's future plans include receiving a degree in Christian Care and Counseling from Oral Roberts University. Hopefully, her next book will include a compilation of her husband's sermons.